NO MORE BULLIES!

Become "bully smart" with this fun activity book, which includes puzzles, mazes, and word searches, plus lots of tips for standing up to bullies!

By Marcia Shoshana Nass

Childswork Childsplay

Secaucus, New Jersey

This book is dedicated to you, the reader. If you are reading this now, you are probably having problems with a bully. But don't worry. After doing the fun activities on the following pages, you'll become "bully smart," and maybe you'll even start a Bully Watch program in your school. If we all stood up to bullies, the world would be a safer, happier place. And you can help make that happen.

© 1998 Childswork/Childsplay, LLC,
  a subsidiary of Genesis Direct, Inc.,
  100 Plaza Drive, Secaucus, NJ 07094.
  1-800-962-1141.
  All rights reserved.

Printed in the United States of America

ISBN # 1-882732-75-8

"Sam, breakfast is ready." It was my mom calling. I dotted some red spots on my face with her lipstick. "Look everyone," I said as I walked into the kitchen. "I've got the chicken pox. I guess I can't go to school."

"Very funny, Sam," said my dad. "You already had the chicken pox."

"Well, I got them again."

"You can only get them once," my mom said.

"Well, I want them again. PLEASE! PLEASE!"

Mom and Dad looked at each other. They thought I had a test that I didn't study for. But I didn't have a test. I had something worse than a test, worse than going to the doctor for a shot. It was even worse than having a piece of spinach stuck in my teeth!

I was having a nightmare. Only this nightmare was happening during the day, and I wasn't sleeping! It was happening five days a week, from 8 to 3—and sometimes even on weekends. My nightmare started the day Horrible Henry moved into the neighborhood.

At first, he just bothered me occasionally. But soon, he was a full-fledged bully. He bullied me so much that I didn't want to go to school.

Do you want to see Horrible Henry? Then finish drawing the picture we've started for you.

Horrible Henry Portrait Puzzle

Yep, that's Horrible Henry all right—though I usually draw horns on him!

Horrible Henry made my life miserable. Unscramble the letters to find out what Henry did to make my life a nightmare. (By the way, try not to peek unless you get stuck, but the answers to the puzzles and games are in the back of this book.)

oret dwarsnig I adem ni ahlf _____

tea ym dnacy _____

aclled em asnty anesm _____

koot ufstf romf em _____

aemd em od sih wemohrok _____

reatthened em _____

barbged ym unhcl _____

tih em metiomses _____

pdsrea rmruos bouta em _____

If someone's bullying you, make a Bully Wheel, like I did, to keep a record. Write down each mean thing the bully does and when. You may need this later. That way, if the bully says, "I never picked on you," you have an exact record, with times and dates.

You're probably good at lots of things, just like me. I won a blue ribbon at the science fair once. I always beat my grandpa at checkers. And I'm good at math and art. My mom always puts my pictures on the refrigerator with little magnets. But I was not good at handling Horrible Henry.

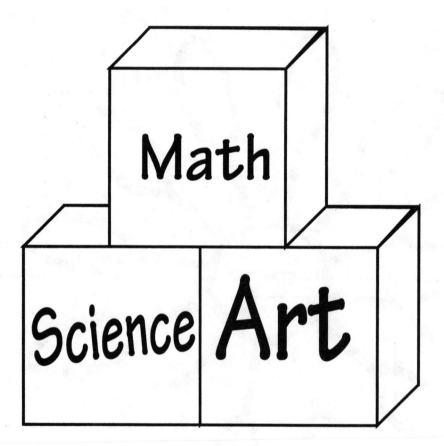

Write down all the things you are good at in the blocks. The sky's the limit. You can build up your blocks as high as you like and keep adding.

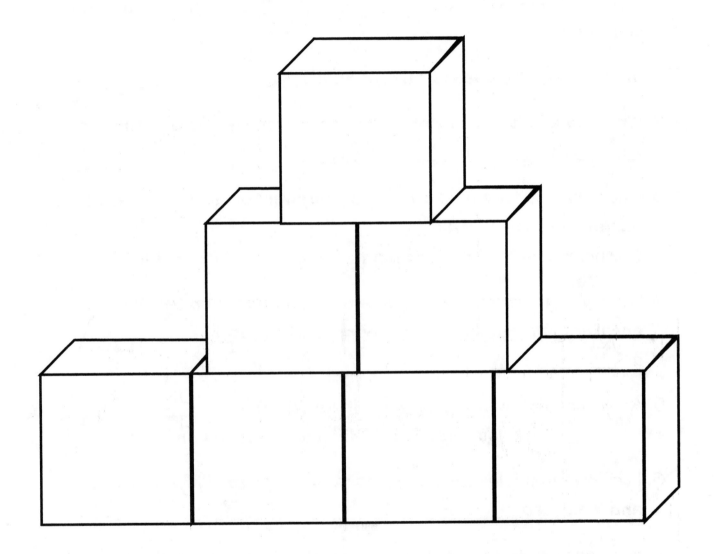

Things we're good at are called our *strengths*. Each new strength usually builds on another one. The things we're not good at are called our *weaknesses*. Sometimes you just need to believe in yourself to develop a new strength. But to believe in yourself, you need something special. To find out what that something special is, first complete the sentences below. Write the letters that land in the stars at the bottom of the page and then rearrange them into one word. Finally, put that word in the sentence given.

1. What a magician does is called a magic ___ ___ ___ ☆ ___ .

2. When I couldn't find any of my things, it was clear it was time to ___ ___ ☆ ___ ___ up my room.

3. Once I had to take music lessons. They were on an instrument that has strings. It's called a ___ ___ ___ ___ ___ ☆ . Our neighbors begged my mom to let me quit. YIPPPEEE!!

4. When you go out in a boat, you are not supposed to catch a sneaker with your line. You are supposed to catch a ☆ ___ ___ ___ .

5. At my cousin's wedding my grandpa said, "Samuel, ☆ ___ ☆ ___ ___ with your grandma." I did, but I stepped on her toes.

6. I tell my mom I don't want to eat it. It looks like a little green tree and it's called ___ ___ ___ ☆ ___ ☆ ___ ___ .

7. Someone needs to korrect this sentense. You can see that I'm not so good at ___ ___ ☆ ___ ___ ☆ ___ ___ .

The secret word is _____ .
I can still have _____ in myself even if I am not good at some things.

8

There are also things we want to be good at. I would like to be good at magic tricks, handling bullies, and telling my parents about Horrible Henry. Write down some of the things you would like to be good at.

BALANCE BEAM OF THINGS TO GET GOOD AT

I wanted to tell my parents about Horrible Henry. I tried, but I just couldn't. I was ashamed. Besides, Horrible Henry threatened to beat me up if I told anyone.

Once he did beat me up, and I looked like this:

BEFORE   **AFTER**

I told my parents I got hurt in soccer.

I really felt bad about hiding my problem from my mom and dad. I made up a word for how I felt: ICKYEEEEUUUUYEEEEEE. It's not a word in the dictionary. It's just my own word. You can tell what it means by the way it sounds.

It's fun to make up words about how you feel. Go ahead–try it. Put your made-up word for how you feel when you've got **Bully Troubles** right here: _____

Can you find these words about how bullies can make you feel? You can go across, down, or diagonally to find them.

WORD SEARCH PUZZLE

```
A N N O Y E D M S R
H N O B F N S A D A
O S G R E E I D U G
R C O R O F C G M E
R A O E Y E K R B R
I R D A C A T D Y O
B E N R U R Z E T T
L D H U R T E B N T
E S I L L Y B A D E
T E R R I B L E P N
```

Words to Find

angry	annoyed	bad	dumb
fear	horrible	hurt	mad
no good	rage	rotten	scared
sick	silly	terrible	

How about making up your own word search puzzle?

First, write down all the words for bullies or the ways they make you feel. Then fill in the letters in horizontally, vertically, or diagonally in the blank grid below. You can do a word search puzzle for any subject and give it to friends to complete.

Bullies want you to think that they are your boss, but remember: YOU ARE YOUR OWN BOSS. Do the crossword puzzle below to see what bullies are like and how they can make you feel like you're not in control.

BOSSWORD PUZZLE

Across

1. Mean, unkind
2. Opposite of nice
3. Opposite of happy
4. Opposite of generous
5. Doesn't tell the truth
6. How someone without friends feels

Down

1. A person who causes trouble
2. Sam's description of Henry

As I was saying, I was feeling ICKYEEEEUUUUYEEEEE most of the time. But that morning when I didn't want to go to school, something changed inside of me.

Have you ever heard the story about the straw that broke the camel's back? My teacher, Ms. James, had told it to us the day before, and something just clicked inside. This is how it goes.

A 🐪 is taking a nice little walk across the desert.

An 🐘 says, "Hey 🐪, can you carry this package across the desert for me?" "Sure," says the 🐪. The 🐘 put the package on the 🐪's back.

A 🦁 says, "Hey 🐪, can you carry my basket of 🍌 across the desert for me?" "Sure," says the camel, and the 🦁 puts the basket on the 🐪's back.

A 🐒 says, "Hey 🐪, can you carry my books across the desert?" "Sure," says the 🐪, and the 🐒 puts the books on the 🐫's back.

The 🐫 was really carrying a heavy burden, and he was

getting angrier and angrier. But he didn't say anything. He just

held his feelings inside.

Finally, a 🐁 says, "Hey 🐫, can you carry this little straw

across the desert? And without even waiting for an answer,

the 🐁 tossed the straw on top of the 🐫's overloaded

back.

The 🐫 shouted, "NO! I AM NOT TAKING ANY OF THIS

STUFF ACROSS THE DESERT. YOU ARE TAKING ADVANTAGE

OF ME, AND I DON'T LIKE IT!"

And that's what happened to me that morning. I had been taking
all of the mean things Horrible Henry did. I did his homework, gave
him money and my favorite cookies, and carried his books. But now I
was afraid to go to school—and I always liked school. Horrible Henry
had pushed me too far.

And like the camel, I started yelling:

I AM NOT GOING TO TAKE THIS ANYMORE. I AM BEING TAKEN ADVANTAGE OF, AND I AM ANGRY.

Have you ever been so, so, *so* ANGRY that you felt you were going to explode? It's like you're a balloon, but instead of being filled with air, you're filled with anger…and you just keep getting bigger and bigger and BIGGER.

Until finally, you're so angry you POP!

In the speech balloons, write what you would like to say to the bully bothering you. Go ahead. Writing what you feel helps get the anger out. No one is going to see it but you.

Do the puzzle on this page to see what Horrible Henry took from me.

STUFFWORD PUZZLE

Across

1. Something to wear when it's cool outside
2. Something to ride that has two wheels
3. What you wear on your feet to play tennis

Down

1. A red fruit
2. Things we play with
3. Something for playing a jumping game

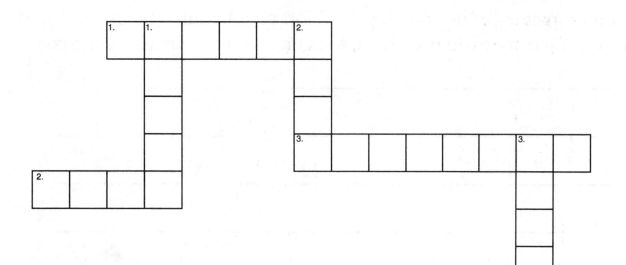

I knew it was time to tell my parents the truth about Henry. Crack the code below to read what I told them.

(Here's the key to figuring out the code. Look at the letters on a computer or a typewriter keyboard. The first letter on the top row of letters is Q, and in this code, Q stands for A. Follow the rest of the alphabet from left to right on the computer, and from the top row to the bottom.)

This is what I said to my parents:

__ _____ _____ ____ __ _____ __

Q WXSSN FQDTR ITFKN OL WGZITKOFU DT.

You can make up your own secret messages to send using this code. I do this with my friend Marty. In code, Marty is spelled: DQKZN. How many names can you spell in code?

Don't forget to list deciphering codes on your building blocks of things you're good at. If you need help, look on the answer page for the code.

_____

_____

_____

_____

This is my parents response to what I told them. Can you figure it out?

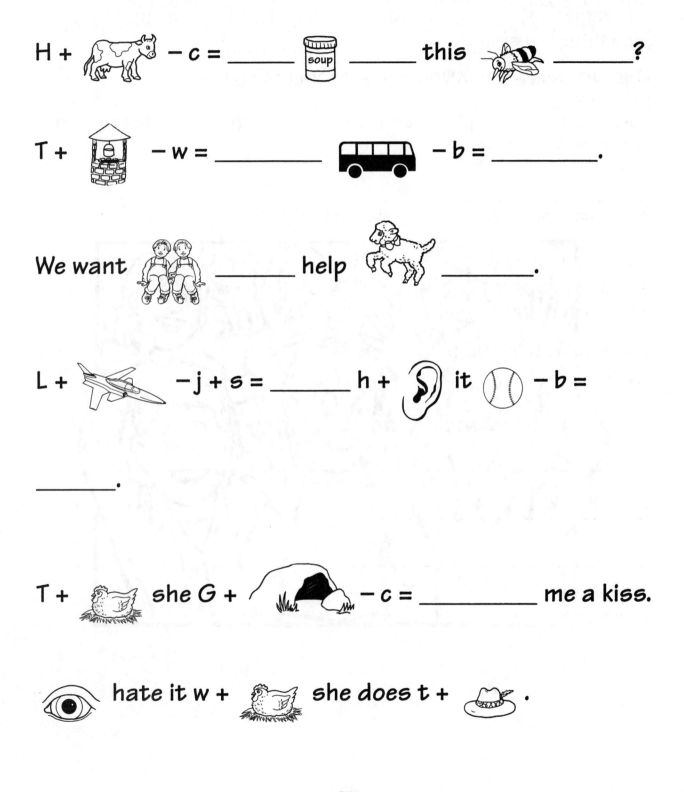

H + 🐄 − c = _____ soup _____ this 🐝 _____?

T + 🏯 − w = _____ 🚌 − b = _____.

We want 👦👦 _____ help 🐑 _____.

L + ✈️ − j + s = _____ h + 👂 it ⚾ − b = _____.

T + 🐔 she G + 🕳 − c = _____ me a kiss.

👁 hate it w + 🐔 she does t + 👒.

After I told Mom and Dad, I felt so much better. Before telling them, I felt like that camel carrying a heavy load, or like that guy, Atlas. Did you ever hear about him? The ancient Greeks believed that he carried the whole world on his shoulders. Mom and Dad also taught me something important:

I DID NOT HAVE TO HANDLE THIS PROBLEM ALONE.

There are always people cheering for you and who are willing to help.

Trust me—if I can learn to stand up to a bully, anyone can! So make this promise to yourself:

I promise to make every effort to stand up to the bully who is bothering me. Completing the activities in this book will help me learn how, and so will telling a trusted adult. I promise on the sun, the moon, and all the stars in the sky.

Name _____

Date _____

Now, who are *you* going to tell about what's happening to you? Write that person's name here. (You can write down the names of more than one person if you want.)

PEOPLE I CAN TELL

_____

_____

_____

_____

_____

Remember, there is no time like the present to stand up to a bully. And learning how to stand up to a bully is the best present you can give to yourself.

In this puzzle, connect the dots. What would you put inside?

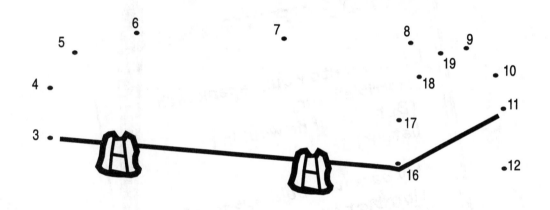

After I told my parents about Henry, my mom said we needed to *brainstorm*. I looked out the window. I knew about snowstorms. That's when you get a day off from school. I knew about rainstorms. There's usually lightning and thunder.

But a brainstorm? I imagined brains falling from the sky and then building a brainman. But a brainstorm isn't like that. Brainstorming is coming up with as many ideas as possible on how to solve a problem. So when you brainstorm, any suggestion is good. Here are some of the ideas we brainstormed.

1. My parents would speak with Horrible Henry.
(But what if he wouldn't listen?)

2. My parents would speak with Horrible Henry's parents.
(But what if they were horrible, too?)

3. Get my cousin Ralph to scare him.
(That was my brainstorm. Ralph is 6 feet tall.)

4. Call the school and speak with Mr. Max, the guidance counselor.

Fill in your own brainstorming ideas.

Now look at your list of solutions. Cross out the ideas you don't think will work. Pick the one you think is best, and plan how to follow through with it.

We decided that the best idea was to have a meeting with Mr. Max, my school guidance counselor. (I still wanted to get my cousin Ralph to scare Henry, but my parents vetoed that idea.) After telling Mr. Max what was happening, he said he knew exactly how I felt. I couldn't believe it. He did? How?

This is what Mr. Max said. It's written in code. Using the key below to substitute the right words for the code words, find out what it says.

"I had a <u>flying pizza</u> chasing me when I was a <u>Martian</u>. The <u>flying pizza's</u> name was Seymour. I remember how it felt. I think that is one of the reasons I became a <u>galactic patrolman</u>—to help other <u>Martians</u> stand up to <u>flying pizzas</u>."

> flying pizza = bully
>
> Martian = kid
>
> galactic patrolman = guidance counselor

"Wow! You had a bully bothering you way back then," I said to Mr. Max. "I guess bullies have been around for a long time."

Mr. Max laughed. "Well, bullies have been around since the days of the dinosaurs."

"Really?" I said.

Mr. Max explained that some dinosaurs were peaceful and just munched on plants. Meat-eating dinosaurs, though, were ferocious and often bullied other dinosaurs—sometimes even eating each other!

Some dinosaurs were dangerous bullies, but others were peaceful. Do you know which was which?

DINOBULLIES CROSSWORD

Across

1. Heaviest dinosaur; stayed in water; ate plants
2. Smallest dinosaur; fast-moving; ate meat; catlike
3. Most feared BULLY of all dinosaurs
4. Plates on back; sharp points on tail; ate plants

Down

1. Long neck; short, dull teeth; ate plants
2. Walked on back legs; ate meat; large claws; sharp teeth
3. Had no teeth; ate fruit, insects, and small animals
4. Giant dinosaur, tiny mouth, ate plants
5. Had a turtlelike shell

Can you answer these riddles Mr. Max told me? The code is based on the multiplication table of 3. The number 3 stands for the letter A, 6 stands for B, 9 stands for C, and so on. Can you decipher them?

T-Rex's mom: **Honey, what refreshments would you like me to get for your birthday party?**

T-Rex: **Oh, don't bother. I'll just ...**

_____ _____ _____ .

15-3-60 39-75 21-63-15-57-60-57

At the party, what would you call a musician with a great beat?

_____ _____ _____ .

3 54-3-48 60-27-36-3

Which dinosaur at the party knew the most words?

The _____ _____ .
   60-24-15 57-3-63-54-63-57

Why is Stegasaurus such a great guest?

Because she always brings her own_____ .
                    48-36-3-60-15-57

What happens to boy or girl dinosaurs after they are 9 years old?

They _____ _____ _____ _____
   60-63-54-42 60-15-42 75-15-3-54-57 45-36-12!

I thought these were pretty funny. Mr. Max is a pretty funny guy. He also told me a Chinese proverb from a famous man named Lao-Tzu. It goes like this: "A journey of a thousand miles must begin with the first step."

I had already taken the first step of my journey by telling my parents about Horrible Henry. I took my second step by telling Mr. Max. Fill in your first two steps.

Mr. Max told me that lots of kids get picked on by bullies. Make believe you are a reporter announcing the latest statistics. See if you can pick the correct numbers from the number square to give an accurate newscast. The numbers can be used more than once.

Numbers to Choose From: 1, 2, 3, 5

The number of bullies is on the rise. At some point in their childhood, _____ in _____ children will face a bully. Children picked on by bullies are ____ times more likely to have stomach aches, _____ times more likely to have headaches, ____ times more likely to have nightmares, ___ times more likely to wet the bed, and are ___ times more likely to feel sad. Bravo to kids who can learn how to stand up to bullies!

And in other news tonight...

It's okay to ask for help in handling a bully. After all, we ask for help for all kinds of other things—when we can't reach the top shelf, if a ball lands in a neighbor's fenced-in yard, with homework, or when we get separated from our parents in a busy store or amusement park. So, if a bully is bothering you, that's a time to ask for help, too.

HELPER WORD GRID

```
D P A R E N T S P
T E A C H E R B O
X G N U R S E Z L
D O C T O R U R I
A C S U I Y Z C C
X W D V X S B D E
P Z X B G U T E M
N E I G H B O R A
S O F I R E M A N
```

Words to Find

dentist	neighbor	policeman
doctor	nurse	teacher
fireman	parents	

Below is a word prism. You can discover what it says by connecting the letters inside with a single line. For example, do you know what these words say?

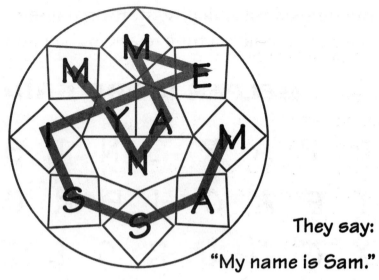

They say:
"My name is Sam."

Now try to connect the letters in the prism below to spell the three word message, which begins, "When I stand up to a bully, I get something money can't buy. I get..."

And you will, too!

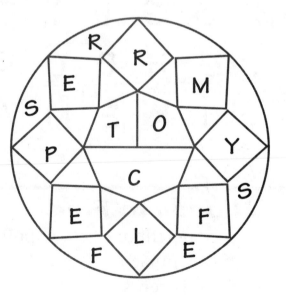

Complete the crossword puzzle to find out what other things help you stand up to a bully.

STRENGTHWORD PUZZLE

Across

1. Something you do again and again in order to improve
2. People you play with and like
3. What someone gives you to help you do something you're afraid to do

Down

1. Have faith in a person; rhymes with fussed
2. What you gain when you're good at something
3. You need this to stand up to a bully
4. The way you feel after standing up to a bully
5. The opposite of weakness

Mr. Max told me I had to learn how to stick up for myself. Sometimes sticking up for yourself means overcoming your fears first. Mr. Max told me something First Lady, Eleanor Roosevelt, once said. (She was married to President Franklin D. Roosevelt.) Unscramble the letters and write the words below to find out what you gain by looking fear in the face.

"You gain TRGHSENT, CROAEUG, and FDCONIECEN by every experience in which you really stop to look fear in the face. You must do the thing you cannot do."

_____

_____

_____

Mr. Max and I started spending lots of time together. I told him about how Horrible Henry made me feel. I even told him about the nightmares I was having. In one nightmare I've had three or four times, I shrink a little each time Horrible Henry bothers me. Eventually, I turn into a little bug.

"Oh, no," I scream in the dream. "What's happening to me?"

"Then what happens?" asked Mr. Max.

I started laughing. "I buzz around Horrible Henry's ear and drive him crazy all day. Sometimes I bite him, and he breaks out all over in an itchy rash."

"So, you would like to torment Horrible Henry?" Mr. Max asked.

"Yeah!" I said.

Mr. Max said it was OK to talk about all the things I thought about doing to get REVENGE on Horrible Henry—as long as I didn't actually do them. Talking about them is called *expressing your anger*.

Another way I expressed my anger was drawing a character I invented called Robo-Ranger. In my fantasy, whenever a bully bothers me, I **click a button hidden in my pocket. The Robo-Ranger gets a laser signal and** instantly appears by my side. He gives the bully a good scare and **sends** him running for the hills.

VAROOOOOM! With one punch, Robo-Ranger can send any bully to the moon. Pretty cool, huh? (I wonder if I could make a million dollars if I could mass produce this and put them on the market???)

My Robo-Ranger didn't always look like this. I erased and redrew him many times in the beginning. He had 4 eyes when I started. Then I erased 2 of them and put 2 times as many back, added 1, multiplied by 4, then divided by 5. By this time, Robo-Ranger had _____ eyes.

At first, Robo-Ranger had a rectangular head. Then I made it into a pentagon, then added 3 new sides. His head was then an _____ .

The Robo-Ranger had 10 antennae, but I multiplied that by 2, then divided by 4, then added 1, subtracted 2, and squared that number. That gave him _____ antennae.

List or draw any ideas you have for a character or invention right here.

_____

Write down the things you would like to do to your bully. Remember, this is just for expressing your anger.

My Bully Revenge List

_____

_____

_____

_____

_____

WA R N I N G: ACTUALLY DOING THE THINGS ON YOUR REVENGE LIST CAN BE HAZARDOUS TO YOUR HEALTH.

The reason for a "Bully Revenge List" is to help you let off steam when you're MAD! See the steam coming out of my ears? I feel much better now.

In some of my nightmares, Horrible Henry becomes a shadow and follows me. Add and subtract the letters to see how I get rid of him.

BURN - b + t + ed= _____

NONE -first n - e = _____

THESE -se =_____

flight - f = _____

And guess what?
The shadow disappears!

But the next day, I almost got stuck sitting next to Horrible Henry in the auditorium. Luckily, I didn't. Can you figure out where I am sitting? And the rest of the people, too?

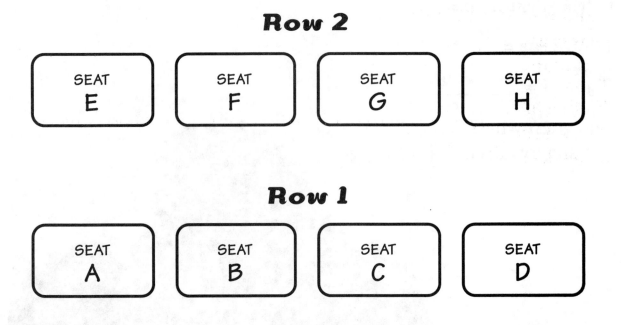

Row 2

| SEAT E | SEAT F | SEAT G | SEAT H |

Row 1

| SEAT A | SEAT B | SEAT C | SEAT D |

1. I am not in seat A.

2. Seat G is broken.

3. Horrible Henry is sitting between my best friend Marty and Eva. Marty likes to sit on the aisle.

4. Marty is not in Seat H.

5. Mrs. Green always sits in Seat D.

6. I like to sit behind Marty because he is short and I can see.

7. Ned got stuck sitting behind Horrible Henry.

8. Jerry hates sitting behind Mrs. Green.

"Bullies like an audience and attention," said Mr. Max. "They want to feel powerful, but deep down they don't feel like they have any control over their lives, so they try to control someone else to feel better."

"Remember the wizard in the *Wizard of Oz*? He had a big loud voice and sounded really scary. But when Dorothy pulled back the curtain, he was just a little man who scared people to make himself feel important."

"Bullies are a little like that," Mr. Max told me. "When you pull back the curtain, you find out that they are frightened and unhappy people who take their fear and loneliness out on others by picking on them."

"But why does he pick me?" I asked.

"One reason" said Mr. Max, "is some kids look more like victims than others do. Bullies seek out these kids first."

Mr. Max told me that to not look like a victim, I would have to stand up tall and put my shoulders back, like I felt good about myself. And I would have to walk confidently and not get all scared if Horrible Henry called me a name, like loser or shorty.

"How do I do that?" I asked.

Unscramble the letters to find out what Mr. Max said.

"By RACINPTICG _____," said Mr. Max.

Eventually, Henry's mean words would just go…That's right! In one ear and out the other.

Mr. Max told me to pretend my mirror was enchanted. I imagined myself bigger and taller and stronger. I imagined myself as a lion. I imagined myself as a superhero. Cool!

Then Mr. Max wanted me to look into the enchanted mirror and say "I love you!" When you look in the mirror, into your own image, you see someone who will always be there for you, someone who will always care about you and be on your side—YOU!

At first I wouldn't do it. "No way!" I said. But then I said I'd try it, as long as he didn't tell any of my friends.

At first, you feel a little goofy. But it REALLY DOES HELP you feel better about things! Try it. You'll really start to feel good about yourself. Don't worry. I won't tell any of your friends.

Remember, check your posture. Are you standing straight? Are your shoulders back? Are you standing proud and tall? Do you look like a WINNER or a victim?

Mr. Max also taught me the right way to talk to myself. Did you realize that we have hundreds of "conversations" with ourselves every day? Sometimes we talk to ourselves in positive ways, but mostly it's negative, like if you forget something and say to yourself, "What a dope!" I had to learn how to change my "negative talk" to "positive talk."

Negative Talk

I am a coward for letting Henry scare me.

I am too short.

I can't do a simple magic trick.

Positive Talk

I am a brave kid for getting help with Henry.

I'm taller than some kids. I'm also nice looking, and when I stand up straight it doesn't matter what my height is.

Magic tricks take practice. Even great magicians, like Houdini, had to practice.

Now turn some of your negative talk into positive things you could say instead:

Negative Talk

_____

_____

_____

_____

Positive Talk

_____

_____

_____

_____

Then Mr. Max taught me how to make *inferences*. That means you infer something, or think about what might happen, from what you already know or see.

Make an inference about each of the following situations. Then decide how you could handle it. The first is done for you, to show what I mean.

Observation:
A bully usually beats me up on the way to school.
I am going to school today.

INFERENCE: <u>If I go to school today, I will be beaten up by the bully.</u>

WHAT CAN I DO? <u>Walk to school with a friend.</u>

Observation:
A bully sometimes harasses me in the bathroom.
I have to go to the bathroom.

INFERENCE: _____

WHAT CAN I DO?

_____

Observation:
A bully in my class always takes my jewelry.
I am wearing jewelry today.

INFERENCE: _____

_____

WHAT CAN I DO? _____

_____

Mr. Max suggested that I not stay alone and feel sorry for myself. Marty has always been my best friend. I started making new friends, too. It was easy to remember their phone numbers, when you realize that each number has three letters attached to it. (Look at the keypad, and you'll see what I mean.) Using some of the letters connected to each number, you can spell out a word of something the person has or likes to do. For example, Marty's number is 276-8437. Marty has a brother.

1	ABC 2	DEF 3
GHI 4	JKL 5	MNO 6
PRS 7	TUV 8	WXY 9
*	0	#

Eva's number is 887-8537. Eva has two _____.
Ned's number is 697-8379. Ned loves a good _____.
Jerry's number is 269-5464. Jerry is great at _____.
Patti's number is 787-7437. Patti has a whole litter of _____ .

My number is 468-3464, and that spells out my favorite magician. Do you know who that is?

Mr. Max said laughter is important. Sometimes a bully can make you feel pretty depressed, so it helps to laugh. In fact, Mr. Max told me that some people believe that laughter can help cure diseases, so I'm sure it can help cure the "Bully Blues!" Below are some of my bully riddles. I hope they make you laugh. I don't recommend, though, telling these to a bully, but you can share them with your best friend.

SAM'S BULLY RIDDLE BOOK

What are a bully's favorite colors?
Black and blue.

What's a bully's favorite food?
Bully-loney sandwiches.

How can you knock a bully down?
With a bully-dozer.

What happened when a bully swallowed a toad?
He became a bully frog.

Did you hear the story about the bully who burped?
Never mind. It's not worth repeating.

If six bullies were all standing under one umbrella, how come none of them got wet?
It wasn't raining!

What happened to the bully frog who was kissed by the princess?
He croaked.

Why did the bully put the banana peel next to his bed?
So he could slip out of bed in the morning.

Why did the bully hit the clock?
Because the clock struck first.

Where did the little bully horse end up when the big bully horse beat him up?
In the horse-pital.

When doesn't a bully feel so hot?
When he has a cold.

What do you say to a bully who is bothering you?
Find out in this knock-knock joke:

Knock, knock.
Who's there?
Leaf.
Leaf who?
Leaf me alone!

Never fight with a bully—unless there's *no choice*. But even if a bully has you cornered, there are some things you can do: pretend you're going to throw up, for example, or pretend you see someone you know. Shout something like, "Oh, Mr. Max! I'm so glad you're here." And when the bully turns around to look, RUN!

"FOOL THE BULLY" WORD SEARCH

```
B  R  U  N  A  W  A  Y  S
L  K  P  Y  E  L  L  E  A
O  I  O  R  Y  E  L  L  Y
W  C  I  Z  E  E  C  L  I
A  K  N  B  Z  R  L  D  S
W  Z  T  X  Y  Z  E  L  E
H  X  S  H  O  U  T  N  E
I  Y  S  C  R  E  A  M  M
S  A  Y  H  E  L  L  O  Y
T  R  U  N  A  W  A  Y  D
L  P  R  E  T  E  N  D  A
E  W  H  I  S  T  L  E  D
```

Words to Find

blow a whistle	whistle	kick	point
run away	say hello	pretend	scream
shout	yell	say I see my dad	

When you insert the right letter into each word in the flowers below, you will spell out a word. The letter will be used 2 times or, in one case, 3 times. Below is an example—my nickname. The missing letter is "m." It is used twice—Sammy. The missing letters are not always used together, but sometimes they are.

Try to figure out these words and see what sentence they form:

FLOWER POWER

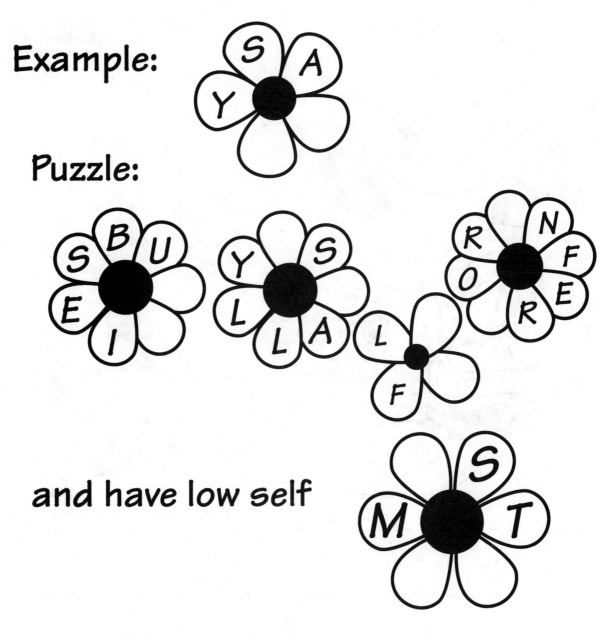

Example:

Puzzle:

and have low self

Mr. Max said I had to start outsmarting Horrible Henry by taking a new way to school.

But Horrible Henry cloned himself on a magic copy machine, and now he's all over the place! Can you find a path from my house to school without my passing Horrible Henry or his 12 clones?

HORRIBLE HENRY X 12

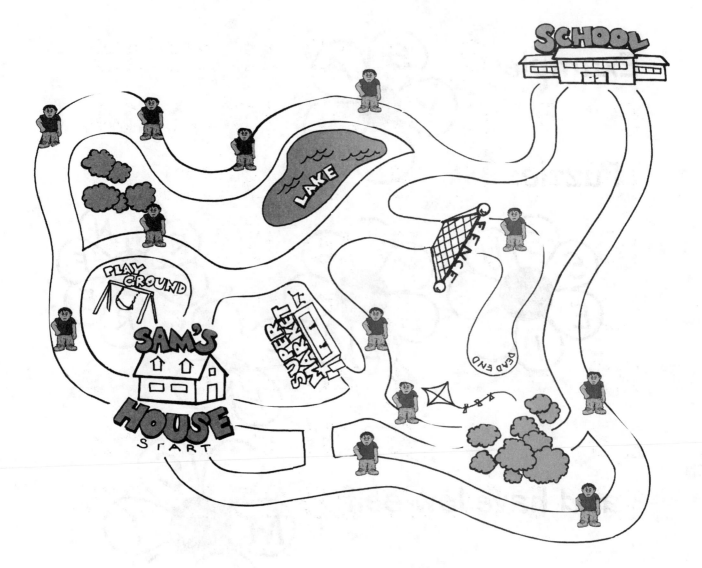

Now Horrible Henry is chasing me through a math maze. How fast can you complete the puzzle to get home? There are several paths, but please take the shortest one! (Going from start to finish, each new square in the path must have a number larger than the previous number in the path.)

MATH MAZE

2	4	6	8	10	11	12	13
9	5	8	4	30	10	11	14
15	5	13	8	9	6	10	15
16	6	14	15	10	8	9	16
18	7	10	5	19	21	22	27
22	8	9	4	29	21	25	30
23	9	6	3	31	6	29	32
24	25	26	27	28	29	31	35

Mr. Max also said I should walk to school with as many friends as I can. You know—safety in numbers.

What's the easiest way for all five of us to go together? *(Hint: some of us can meet at each other's house, but we can only do that twice.)*

FRIENDS MAZE

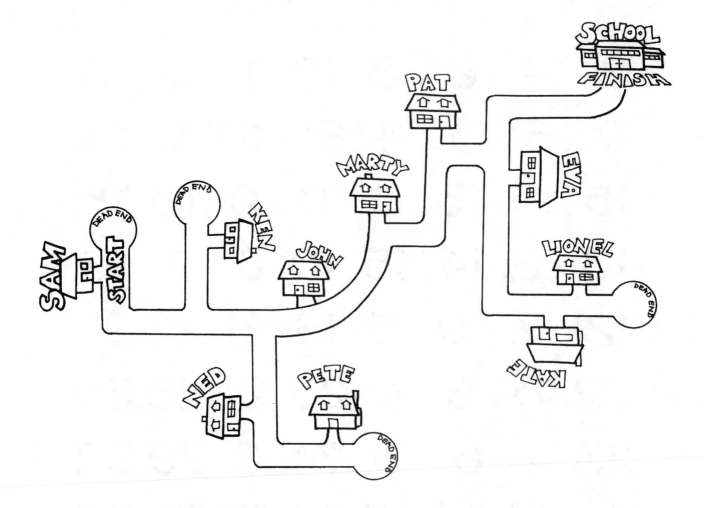

You're doing something good for yourself—and for your species—when you stand up to a bully. If bullies took over the world, and there was even more violence, humans might become an endangered species, like the rhinoceros, snow leopard, Asiatic lion, Indian elephant, and little blue Macao.

Many people (and I agree with them!) feel that we must protect endangered animals, or many species could become extinct. We should also help each other stand up to bullies, right? I mean, we're a species, too, aren't we? Do you know what species we belong to? Use the key to decipher the code:

It means wise and intelligent—another word for humankind.

Another way to get rid of fears is to just to let them float away. Write your fears in the empty balloons on this page, then imagine them drifting into the sky. Say: "As I let this balloon go, my fear is leaving me."

Fear of being embarassed

Fear of being hurt

Many people don't really know the truth about bullies. In fact, if you were a contestant on the "No More Bullies Game Show," how would you score? Give yourself 10 points for each correct answer.

BULLY TRUE/FALSE TEST

True or False?

1. Bullies are extremely well-liked and popular.

2. Young bullies watch a lot of violent TV and cartoons.

3. Bullies need help as much as their victims do.

4. Most bullies are seeking power and attention.

5. Many bullies are being bullied by someone at home.

6. If young bullies don't get help, they may eventually wind up in jail or in serious trouble.

7. Bullies are brave and have high self-esteem.

8. Bullies choose victims who they think are weak.

9. Bullies can stop bullying in about 3-4 days once they get help.

10. Many bullies are lonely and unhappy people.

A score of 80-100 means you are a Gold Star Bully Expert; 50-70 a Silver Star Bully Expert, and 30-40 a Bronze Star Bully Expert. Below that, you need to study up!

Did I tell you about my Aunt Jane? She's visually challenged and reads in Braille. She won a medal in the Special Olympics and also came in second in a marathon race. She can do anything! That's because she believes in herself.

Many people just see obstacles as challenges to overcome. Beethoven, a brilliant composer, was deaf, and Thomas Edison (who discovered the light bulb and thousands of other things) had a learning disability. (I'm glad he invented that light bulb, or I'd have to go to bed even earlier than I do now!)

James Earl Jones, who was Darth Vader in one of my favorite movies, *Star Wars*, stuttered as a child, and when Harrison Ford ("Indiana Jones") was a little kid, he was picked on by a bully.

So, instead of feeling bad if a bully is picking on you, see it as a challenge—a challenge you will overcome if you just

_____

Insert the circled letters from the Braille alphabet here and unscramble them. Some will be used more than once.

Try writing your name in Braille below. You can even make your own Braille alphabet. Just glue little dried peas or beans on cardboard and practice feeling the letters. If you learn to write in Braille, you can add that to your blocks of things you're good at.

Braille Alphabet

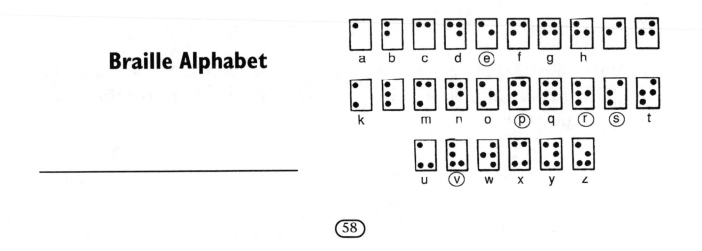

_____

Native Americans have great respect for nature and animals. They believe we are all connected in something they call the Great Web of Life. Many of them take names that compare them with the land, birds, trees, animals, or forces of nature. They have names like Crashing Thunder and Mountain Stream.

Can you unscramble these Native American names?

ZARCY ORHSE _____

NNNIURG OKORB_____

TISTIGN LUBL _____

AGEEL RTSA _____

NUHDERT DCLUO_____

NADCING EARB _____

ISRIGN UNS _____

EWETS TAWER _____

I gave myself a name: IGHNLTING ALFSH. What Native American name would you give yourself?

By the way, the Coyote is celebrated in many Indian songs. It is a symbol of not taking things too seriously.

For this exercise, can you figure out what the items in each of these groups have in common?

Glass, aluminum, newspapers, plastic _____

Bach, Mozart, Beethoven, Chopin _____

Prunes, olives, peaches, nectarines, watermelon _____

Georgia O'Keefe, Picasso, Manet, Cezanne, Van Gogh

_____

32, 65, 131, 263 _____

John Adams, Herbert Hoover, Franklin D. Roosevelt

_____

Asteroid, comet, meteor, nebulae _____

Sharks, seaweed, jellyfish, coral reefs, icebergs

_____

Take lunch money, make threats, tease, taunt, hurt you

_____

Mr. Max taught me that NO! can be a complete sentence. You don't have to say anything else. If a bully says, "Give me your lunch," you just say "No" and walk away!

Practice saying, "NO, NO, NO, NO, NO." Just say "No" and then "go."

Set a timer for 5 minutes. See how many words you can list with the word "no" in them in that time. Have a contest with a friend.

Hey! Listen to this rap song I wrote about Henry:

I used to think Horrible Henry was really C O O L,
But now I know he was just a F O O L.

He picked on me cause I'm kinda S M A L L,
But now I feel ten feet T A L L!

I can stand up to him, I know I C A N,
From now on I'm my number one F A N!

Write a rap song about your bully. Rhyme the last words on lines 1 and 2, 3 and 4, and 5 and 6. Then put on your shades and rap around the house.

Sometimes, when I went to the bathroom, Horrible Henry was there, and he'd take some of my money to buy his lunch. I tried not to go to the bathroom at school, but it was hard!

Henry would always buy chicken on a roll, with a soda, fries, and pie. If I had only $5.00 with me, what could I afford to buy myself after Henry had taken my money?

MENU

Chicken on a roll	$2.00
Turkey	$2.25
Roast beef	$3.00
Pizza	$1.25
Fries	$ .50
Spinach (Yuk!)	$1.50
Soda	$1.00
Apple juice	$ .50
Pie	$ .50

One day, Henry said, "Get me chicken on a roll." And I took out a picture like the one here and gave it to him. I thought that was pretty funny. Horrible Henry didn't laugh. He got even madder. Now I just say "No" and walk away.

Mr. Max finally got Horrible Henry to meet with him. Just like Mr. Max thought, Henry had lots of anger in him. Finally, Mr. Max had Horrible Henry and me in his office together. That's when I found out that the big bully's dad always yelled at him and sometimes hit him. His mom was very sick in the hospital, and his dad was out of work.

Mr. Max said these were not an excuse for bullying me. After that I thought Horrible Henry would stop bothering me. But he didn't.

In fact, the next day Horrible Henry said, "Sam, give me your bike." I said "NO!" and walked away. I held my head high and spoke in a loud, firm voice, like I had practiced in front of the mirror.

Horrible Henry looked surprised. Then he walked away and didn't bother me the rest of the day. But that afternoon, my bike was missing. I knew Horrible Henry had taken it.

Mr. Max asked lots of kids if they had seen my bike. He asked Horrible Henry, too, but Henry said he didn't know anything about it. I knew he was lying, but how could I prove it?

Later that afternoon, my friends Marty, Ned, and I were playing ball in the park. Marty threw Ned a ball, and Ned missed. (Ned **always misses**.) We looked under some bushes for it, and guess what we **discovered**?

"Look! It's your bike, Sam," shouted Marty.

"Whoever took it must have been afraid of getting caught," I said.

"Don't touch it," Ned warned. "It may have a fresh fingerprint on it."

Ned had read all the Inspector Truth stories from the *Super Sleuth* detective book series. He was a member of the Super Sleuth Detective Club and had earned a gold badge. It wasn't real gold, but Ned insisted it was, so we pretended we believed him.

Here are some of the cases Ned read about. See if you can solve them.

#1. A man named Shannu was considered the smartest person in the land. This upset the Queen, who wanted to prove to the people that she was smarter. One day, she figured out a way to outsmart Shannu. She drew a line in the sand and said, "Shannu, you must make this line shorter, but you cannot erase any of the line. Do you understand? The Queen smiled. The people applauded. She had finally stumped Shannu. But Shannu laughed. He knew exactly what to do.

_____

Can you make this line shorter?

#2. An FBI agent's husband told me how his wife died of a heart attack in her sleep—the victim of an incredibly scary dream. She was caught by enemy agents and was about to be thrown into a lake of man-eating sharks.

What's wrong with this story? Write your answer below.

_____
_____
_____
_____
_____
_____.

It took me a while to figure these out.

"But what should we do about the bicycle, Ned?" asked Marty.

"Please call me Detective Ned when I'm working," said Ned. He'd been waiting his whole life for something like this.

Ned said he was going to check the bike for fingerprints. He ran home and got his Super Sleuth Detective Kit. He examined the bike with his magnifying glass.

"Look!" he said. Marty and I took turns looking—it was a fresh thumbprint!

Ned showed us how to take a print off an object. There are fingerprint powders made especially for crime detection, but sometimes you can use plain white talcum powder if the surface is metal and a dark color, like my bike. We lifted the thumbprint off the bike and put it on the special crime detection paper that came with Ned's kit. This is what it looked like:

"Now all we have to do is find out whose thumbprint matches," said Ned—I mean Detective Ned. We brought the evidence to Mr. Max. Ned brought his Super Sleuth paint into school. All the kids allowed Ned to take their prints. They put their thumbs in the paint and then pressed down on Ned's coded paper.

Can you tell whose thumbprint matched the one on my bike? Just as I thought! It belonged to Horrible Henry!

Henry

Ned

Betsy

Eva

Marty

Now I had Horrible Henry just where I wanted him. Stealing is against the law. Oh, boy! Was he ever going to get into trouble. I was going to nail him!

"Ha, ha! Horrible Henry, I got you now," I told him. "I finally got you just where I want you. I'm going to call the police, and then they'll call your father. Maybe he'll tell them to put you in reform school or jail or …"

But then the craziest thing happened. You'll never believe it. Horrible Henry started crying. He cried so much this page got soaked from his tears.

Then I thought about Henry and his father—and his mother sick in the hospital. I thought about Henry's father hitting him and I said, "Well, maybe I'll give you another chance."

Horrible Henry gaped at me. He couldn't believe it. "Why would you help me?" he asked.

"I have no idea," I said.

Horrible Henry never said thanks. But I think he wanted to.

Mr. Max said, "I'm proud of you, Sam. You've shown ISOMPACSON and SNVGOFRIEES for Horrible Henry."

Unscramble the letters to find out what Mr. Max said I had shown.

_____

and

_____

Mr. Max told me something that the civil rights leader, Martin Luther King, Jr., said: "Forgiveness is not an occasional act. It is a permanent attitude."

I don't know if I could ever be like Dr. King and have a permanent attitude of forgiveness. But I do know that on that day, I forgave Horrible Henry. I even started calling him Henry.

The next day at school was Friendship Day. Everyone brought in pictures of their best friends. I brought in one of Marty when his front tooth was missing. Everyone laughed.

When it was Henry's turn, he just sat there.

"Henry, do you have a picture of your best friend?" asked Ms. James.

Henry just stared straight ahead. "No," he said.

"Why not?" asked Ms. James.

"I don't have any friends," said Henry.

That afternoon, I invited Henry over to my house. We played some computer games. Here's one game we played:

Each square had to be connected to the triangle with the same face, but no line could cross another. Can you do it?

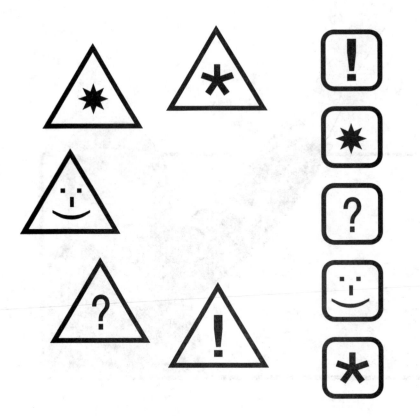

Henry was really good at it. It took me a while to figure it out. Then we played some other games.

Henry asked if I had a camera. He wanted to take a picture of me. "You're my best friend," he said.

"I am?" I said. I couldn't believe it.

"Yeah," he muttered. "Well actually, you're my only friend." Then we both laughed. I'd never heard Henry laugh before.

Henry had lots of counseling sessions with Mr. Max. He also went to see the school social worker and a private psychologist during the week. My other friends didn't like Henry too much, because he was kind of bossy, but I still played with him.

But then one day I noticed that Henry wasn't in school.

"What happened to Henry?" I asked Mr. Max.

"Henry has gone to live with his Aunt Bess and will be going to a school in the next district. Everyone agreed that would be the best thing until his father gets help and stops taking his anger out on Henry."

That's when I learned what a *vicious cycle* is. Henry's father had problems and took them out on Henry. And then Henry took his anger out on me.

"But he didn't even say good-bye," I told Mr. Max.

"He left you this." I read the letter Mr. Max handed me.
This is what it said:

Dear Sam,

I am sorry for all the times I was mean to you. Thanks for being my friend.

Maybe someday I can come and visit. If you want me to.

Henry

"Sam, you're a hero," said Mr. Max. "You not only helped yourself out, but you ended up helping out Henry and his dad, too. They're getting the help they need now because you had the courage to come forward."

"A hero? Me? Wow!"

I read up about other heroes. Can you match these heroes and their accomplishments?

 **Heroes**

ALBERT EINSTEIN

MARTIN LUTHER KING, JR.

MAHATMA GHANDI

JIM THORPE

CHARLES ALEXANDER EASTMAN

MARY MCLEOD BETHUNE

GEORGE WASHINGTON CARVER

FLORENCE NIGHTINGALE

ANDREW CARNEGIE

DAG HAMMARSKJOLD

BESSIE COLEMAN

NELSON MANDELLA

HARRIET TUBMAN

JOHN GLENN

MARIE CURIE

Accomplishments

Female physicist and chemist

Nurse

Former Secretary General of the United Nations

Teacher and female civil rights activist

Preacher, famous civil rights leader

Native American athlete

Philanthropist, American industrialist

1st black female pilot and aviator

Black botanist

Black South African president

Headed Underground Railroad

Astronaut

Physician-writer

Famous scientist ($E = mc^2$)

Won his country independence through non-violent demonstrations

I decided to write myself a poem. This is it:

I don't need wings,
I don't have to fly,
I'm my own superhero
I'm telling you why.
I stood up to a bully,
It wasn't easy to do,
And when it was over
I helped him, too.

You can write a poem, too, or maybe keep a record of your feelings in a journal or diary. Or how about writing a letter to the future kids of Planet Earth? Tell them what happened to you and the bully you stood up to. If you bury the letter in your backyard, it will be a time-capsule letter.

You can start your letter off something like this:

To the Kids of the Future:

I thought you might like to know what is happening to a kid my age in these days in the year _____.

Pat yourself on the back. When you stand up to a bully, you are a hero. I mean it. You are doing something great.

Connect the dots to form something special, then put your name in it.

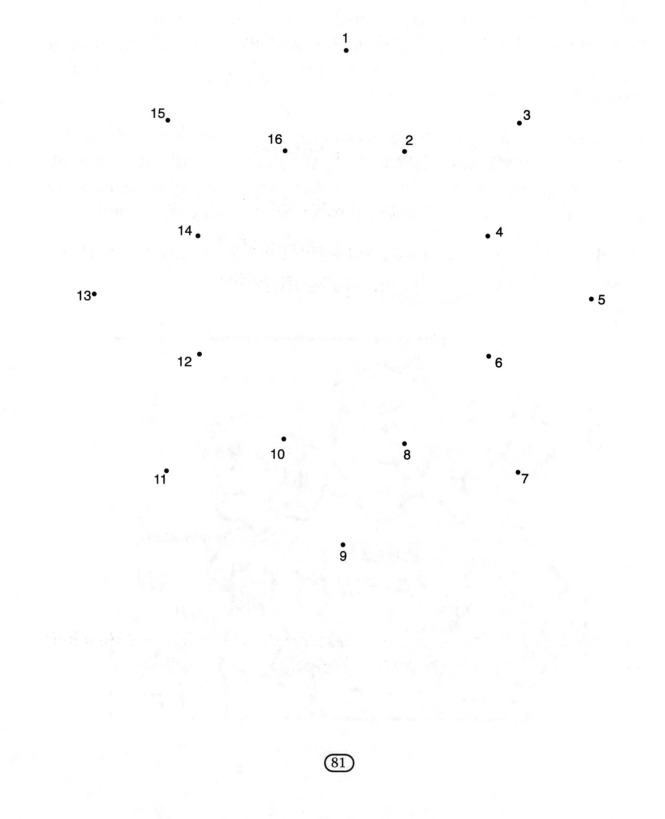

One more thing: Mr. Max and I started a BULLY PROOF WATCH program. It's based on kids having the right to study, learn, have fun and be safe at school and in their neighborhoods without being bothered by any bullies.

The kids all got together and formed a Bully Watch Committee. If a bully picks on someone, all the kids in the Bully Watch Committee go together to give him or her a Bully Summons, which is immediately reported to the school principal.

We posted "No Bullying Zone" signs around the neighborhood and established Bully Patrols to make sure the hallways and bathrooms at school would be safe from bullies. Bullies can't win anymore, because the kids in our school are sticking up for each other against bullies.

The parents and Parent Teacher's Association got involved, too. Our whole town has now taken a stand against bullying!

My grandmother always said that something good can come out of something bad. Out of my bad situation with Henry, our school is now becoming bully proof, and I am the one who started it. I'm kind of proud of myself.

There are other times when bad things turned into good for me, too. Once it rained so hard, I couldn't' go out and play with my friends. I was upset. But then my dad came home early and taught me how to play chess.

Can you think of a time when something bad turned into good. If so, write it here:

_____

_____

Even the word *bully* can be turned into something good:

    B = Believe in yourself.

    U = Understand being picked on is not your fault.

    L = Love yourself.

    L = Love yourself a little more.

    Y = You can do it. I believe in you.

Dr. Max keeps a sign on his door with a quote from a famous anthropologist named Margaret Mead. This is what it says:

> **"Never doubt that a small group of concerned people can change the world. Indeed, it is the only thing that ever has."**

If you want to become part of a small group of people who can change the world, start a Bully Watch program at your school. When kids help each other, amazing things begin to happen. It's almost like magic.

Insert a picture of yourself below.

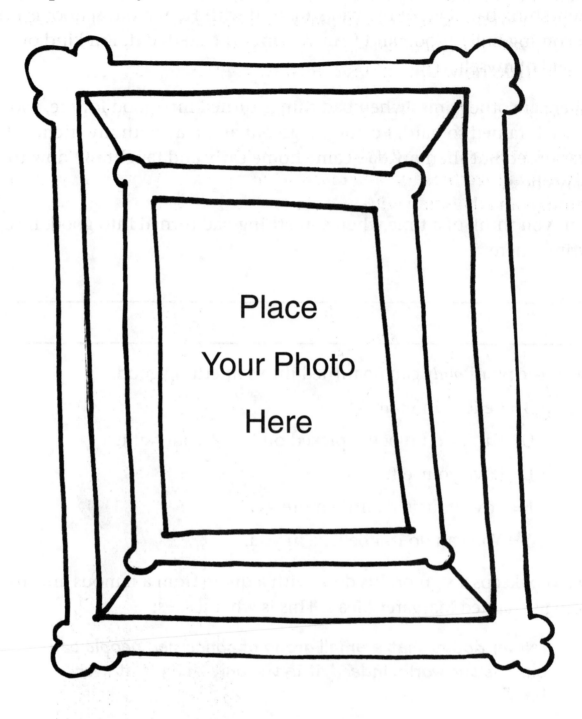

Place

Your Photo

Here

I STOOD UP TO A BULLY

Once the problem with Henry was settled, I had more confidence in myself. I even learned how to make a quarter appear out of someone's ear. It's called *sleight of hand*. I'm pretty good at it. I can do lots of magic tricks now. Uh, oh! I just made myself disappear.

Oh! Here I am again. Now I'm standing on top of the world.

Well, it was nice talking with you. I feel like we've gone through an adventure together, and you know what they say? Whenever you go through an adventure with someone, you are friends forever.

ANSWER KEY

page 4

tore drawings I made in half
ate my candy
called me nasty names
took stuff from me
made me do his homework
threatened me
grabbed my lunch
hit me sometimes
spread rumors about me

page 8

trick
clean
violin
fish
dance
broccoli
spelling

SECRET WORD:
CENFDNCOEI
(confidence)

page 11— Wordsearch Grid

page 13—Bossword Puzzle

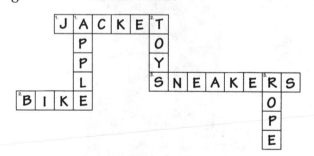

page 19 —Stuffword Puzzle

page 20 — Q=A, W=B, E=C, R=D, T=E, Y=F, U=G, I=H, O=I, P=J
         A=K, S=L, D=M, F=N, G=O, H=P, J=Q, K=R, L=S,
         Z=T, X=U, C=V, V=W, B=X, N=Y, M=Z
         (A bully named Henry is bothering me.)

page 21 — How can this be?
Tell us.
We want to help you.
Let's hear it all.
Then she gave me a kiss.
I hate it when she does that!

page 25 — TREASURE CHEST

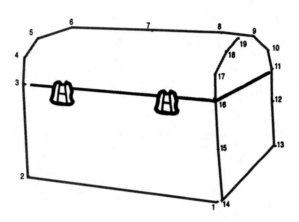

page 28 — I had a bully chasing me when I was a kid. **The bully's name was Seymour. I** remember how it felt. It think that is one of the **reasons I became a guidance** counselor—to help other kids stand up to bullies.

page 29 — Dinobullies Crossword

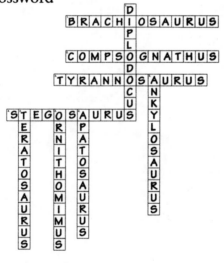

page 30 — Eat my guests.
A rap-tile
The-saurus
Plates.
They turn ten years old.

page 32 —— 1, 5, 2, 2, 3, 2, 3

page 33 — Helper Word Grid

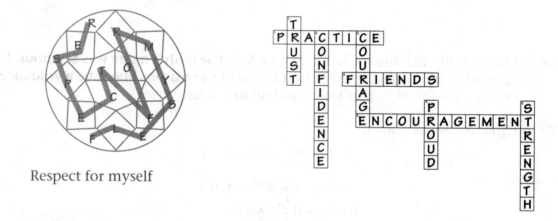

D	P	A	R	E	N	T	S	P
T	E	A	C	H	E	R	B	O
X	G	N	U	R	S	E	Z	L
D	O	C	T	O	R	U	R	I
A	C	S	U	I	Y	Z	C	C
X	W	D	V	X	S	B	D	E
P	Z	X	B	G	U	T	E	M
N	E	I	G	H	B	O	R	A
S	O	F	I	R	E	M	A	N

page 34

Respect for myself

page 35 — Strengthword Puzzle

page 36 — strength, courage, confidence

page 39 — 4 eyes
         octogan
         16 antennae

page 41 — turned on the light

page 42 — Seat E: Sam   Seat F: Ned   Seat G: broken seat   Seat H: Jerry
          Seat A: Marty   Seat B: Horrible Henry   Seat C: Eva   Seat D: Mrs. Green.

page 44 — practicing

page 47 — INFERENCE: I may get beaten up.
            TO DO: I can go with my friends or take different route.
            INFERENCE: Bully may find me alone in bathroom.
            TO DO: Go to bathroom with a classmate.
            INFERENCE: Bully may take my jewelry
            TO DO: Don't wear jewelry to school.

page 48 — Eva has two turtles.
            Ned loves a good mystery.
            Jerry is great at bowling.
            Patti has a whole litter of puppies.
            My favorite magician is Houdini.

page 50 — Fool The Bully Wordsearch

page 51 — In the flowers it says, "Bullies usually feel inferior and have low self esteem."

page 52 — Horrible Henry Puzzle x12

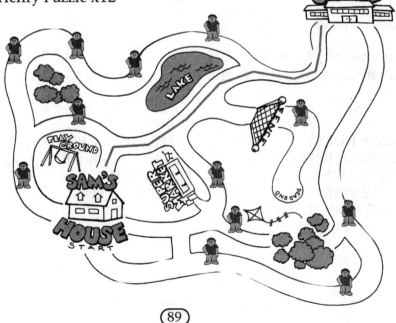

page 53 — MATH MAZE

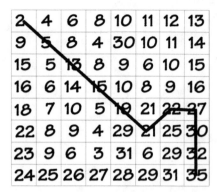

page 54 — FRIENDS MAZE

Pete, Ned, and Ken meet at John's house. Sam meets them at John's, and they all continue walking to school, picking up Marty and then Pat along the way. Meanwhile, Kate and Lionel meet at Eva's, Sam and his pals pick them up there, and everyone continues to school.

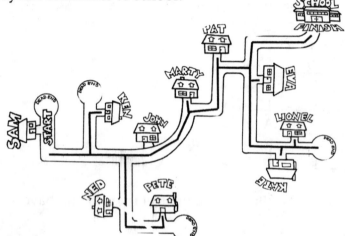

page 55 — Homo sapiens

page 57 — Statements 1, 7, and 9 are false.
Statements 2, 3, 4, 5, 6, 8, and 10 are true.

page 58 — persevere

page 59 — CRAZY HORSE   THUNDER CLOUD
RUNNING BROOK   DANCING BEAR
SITTING BULL   RISING SUN
EAGLE STAR   SWEET WATER
LIGHTNING FLASH

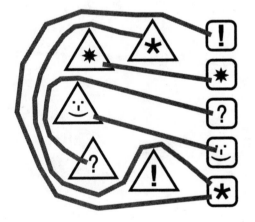

page 78

ALBERT EINSTEIN — Female physicist and chemist

MARTIN LUTHER KING, JR. — Nurse

MAHATMA GHANDI — Former Secretary General of the United Nations

JIM THORPE — Teacher and female civil rights activist

CHARLES ALEXANDER EASTMAN — Preacher, famous civil rights leader

MARY MCLEOD BETHUNE — Native American athlete

GEORGE WASHINGTON CARVER — Philanthropist, American industrialist

FLORENCE NIGHTINGALE — 1st black female pilot and aviator

ANDREW CARNEGIE — Black botanist

DAG HAMMARSKJOLD — Black South African president

BESSIE COLEMAN — Headed Underground Railroad

NELSON MANDELLA — Astronaut

HARRIET TUBMAN — Physician-writer

JOHN GLENN — Famous scientist ($E = mc^2$)

MARIE CURIE — Won his country independence through non-violent demonstrations

page 81 — Star

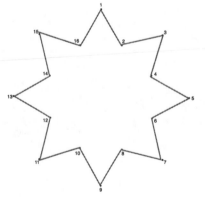

NOTES

ABOUT THE AUTHOR

Marcia Shoshana Nass is a writer for children and the author of the nationally acclaimed "Songs for Peacemakers" program endorsed by the National School Safety Center, National Education Association, and National Crime Prevention Council. She is also the co-creator of the *No More Bullies* game, "Kindness Makes the World A Happy Place," and "Mediation for Little Peacemakers." She teaches reading and writing at the Prodigy Academy in Queens, New York, and has won numerous awards for her educational programs.

This activity book is based on a child who had a problem with a bully. And like Sam, Nass's husband Max also had a problem with a bully when he was young. Max Nass is now a guidance counselor.